HOLICH

# STAR WARS

## CLONE WARS
### ADVENTURES
#### VOLUME 9

D0995094

designers
**Darin Fabrick and Josh Elliott**

assistant editor
**Dave Marshall**

editor
**Jeremy Barlow**

publisher
**Mike Richardson**

special thanks to Elaine Mederer, Jann Moorhead,
David Anderman, Leland Chee, Sue Rostoni, and
Amy Gary at Lucas Licensing

The events in these stories take place sometime
during the Clone Wars.

www.titanbooks.com

www.starwars.com

**STAR WARS: CLONE WARS ADVENTURES** Volume 9, December 2007.
Published by Titan Books, a division of Titan Publishing Group Ltd., 144 Southwark
Street, London SE1 0UP. Star Wars ©2007 Lucasfilm Ltd. & ™. All rights reserved.
Used under authorization. Text and illustrations for Star Wars are © 2007 Lucasfilm
Ltd. No portion of this publication may be reproduced or transmitted, in any form or
by any means, without the express written permission of the copyright holder. Names,
characters, places, and incidents featured in this publication either are the product of
the author's imagination or are used fictitiously. Any resemblance to actual persons
(living or dead), events, institutions, or locales, without satiric intent, is coincidental.
PRINTED IN ITALY

2 4 6 8 10 9 7 5 3 1

# CLONE WARS

ADVENTURES

## VOLUME 9

**"APPETITE FOR ADVENTURE"**
script and art **The Fillbach Brothers**
colors **Ronda Pattison**

**"SALVAGED"**
script and art **The Fillbach Brothers**
colors **Pamela Rambo**

**"LIFE BELOW"**
script and art **The Fillbach Brothers**
colors **Dan Jackson**
with Madigan Jackson

**"NO WAY OUT"**
script and art **The Fillbach Brothers**
colors **Tony Avina**

lettering
**Michael Heisler**

cover
**The Fillbach Brothers and Dan Jackson**

A CLONE WARS
DEXTER JETTSTER in
**APPETITE FOR ADVENTURE**
ADVENTURE

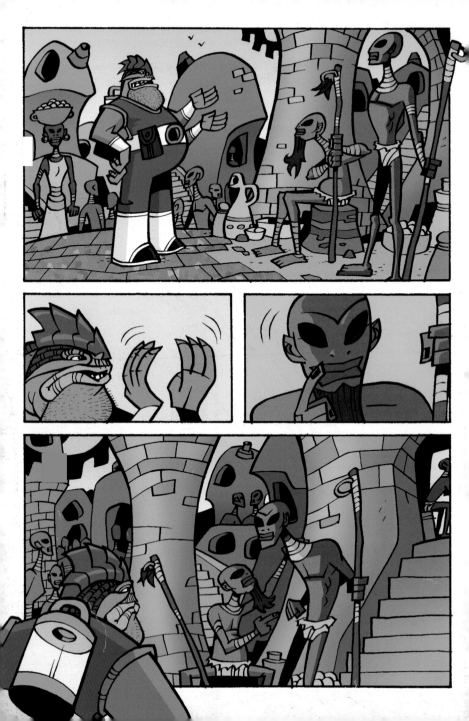

SKREEEE!!!

SMAK!

YEE-YOR!!

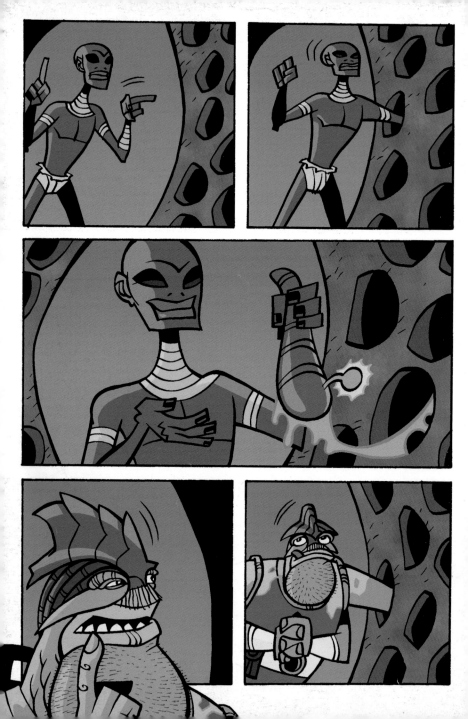

**splish!**

WE HAVE A PROBLEM, SIR...

...A CLONE TROOPER'S LIFE SUPPORT SYSTEM IS STILL ACTIVE, BUT AT CRITICAL. WHAT ARE THE INSTRUCTIONS?

→sigh← TAKE HIM TO SICK BAY... AY-YI-YI.

LOOK AT THIS MESS! YOU STUPID CLONE...DO YOU KNOW HOW LONG IT TOOK ME TO REPROGRAM THOSE DROIDS?! *SHEESH!*

UH...

IT'S JUST AN *ELECTRO-DART.* DON'T BE SUCH A BABY. *FEH!* YOU CLONES DON'T SEEM THAT TOUGH TO ME.

NOW, I DIDN'T WANT TO HAVE TO DO THIS, BUT YOU LEAVE ME NO CHOICE... GIVE ME YOUR LEG!

SEE? I FEEL MUCH SAFER NOW... DON'T YOU?

WHAT DO YOU WANT, OLD MAN?

NAME'S *HURD COYLE.* I SAVED YER BUTT WHEN I SALVAGED YOUR STARFIGHTER. YOU CLONES MUST BE PRETTY BUSY KILLING ALLA THEM *JEDI* WITH *ORDER 66,* EH?

*WHAT?*

YOU HAVEN'T HEARD? THE JEDI ARE NOW YOUR ENEMIES.

*ORDER 66?!* WHEN DID THIS HAPPEN?

*HA!* YOU GO OFF FLOATING AROUND IN SPACE FOR A FEW WEEKS AND YOU MISS OUT ON YOUR ORDERS, *EH,* CLONE? I'VE GOT DROIDS TO REPAIR. BYE.

pling!

tink!

WHAT HAS HIT MY FOOT?

YOUR RETIREMENT!

KOOM!

HELLO AND WELCOME! HOW MAY I SERVE YOU TODAY, GOOD SIRS?

THESE OLD SHIPS HAVE BEEN TRANSPORTING JEDI TO HIDE THEM IN THE OUTER RIM TERRITORIES... TEAR THE PLACE APART, MEN.

*UH...*I'M A SIMPLE SALVAGE SHIP CAPTAIN! *PLEASE,* THIS IS *ALL* I HAVE!

COMMANDER!

I'M SUNK.

I'M HOB-147 OF THE LIGHT BRIGADE DIVISION. CAPTAIN COYLE SALVAGED MY SHIP AND SAVED ME.

I'VE BEEN UP AND DOWN THIS VESSEL AND IT'S AS THE CAPTAIN SAID...A SIMPLE SALVAGE SHIP.

**QUINLAN VOS,** QUITE HORRIBLE YOU LOOK...

...AND **WORSE** YOU SMELL.

TRUDGING THROUGH THE SEWERS FOR THE PAST WEEK WAS NO PICNIC, MASTER.

YOUR MISSION, A SUCCESS IT WAS?

YES AND NO.

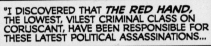

"I DISCOVERED THAT *THE RED HAND*, THE LOWEST, VILEST CRIMINAL CLASS ON CORUSCANT, HAVE BEEN RESPONSIBLE FOR THESE LATEST POLITICAL ASSASSINATIONS...

"LED BY THE DEADLY *AYO MOROTA*, THE RED HAND HAS BEEN USING THE UNDER-GROUND SEWER SYSTEM AS A BASE OF OPERATIONS."

*HMM.* QUITE CLEVER, ACCESS TO THE ENTIRE CITY THEY WOULD HAVE. CONTINUE.

I INFILTRATED THEIR ORGANIZATION TO FIND OUT WHO IS GIVING THEM ORDERS ...WHO IS *REALLY* IN CONTROL.

I WAS CLOSE TO FINDING OUT TOO. BUT MY DECEPTION TURNED RATHER... WELL...

EXECUTIONERS!!

COME ON, GUYS. WE HAD SOME GOOD TIMES, RIGHT? CUT ME SOME SLACK.

OH, WE'LL DO MORE THAN CUT YOU SLACK, QUIN.

I GOT HIM! I GOT HIM!!

AAAH!

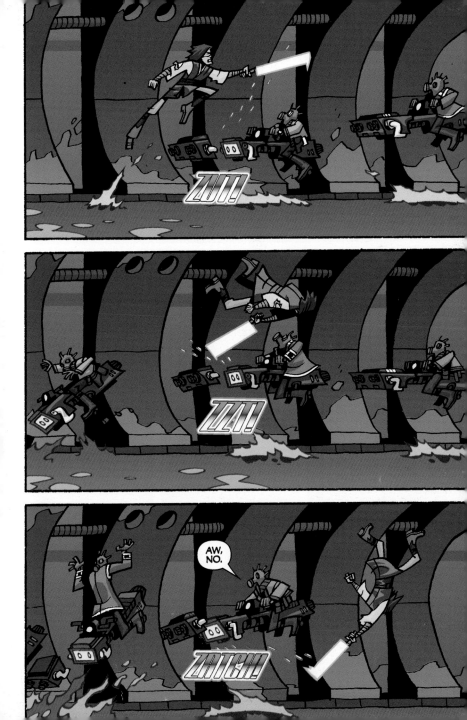

BWOOOM!

OH, YES.

NOW LET'S SEE...A LEFT. A RIGHT. ANOTHER LEFT...

UP THREE JUNCTIONS... AND THEN...

...I THINK I'M LOST.

HE'S AT JUNCTION SEVEN! THE REST OF YOU COME WITH ME!

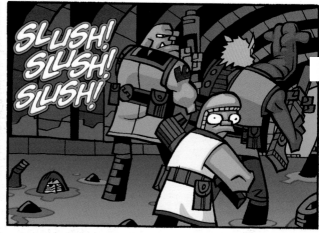

THERE'S NOWHERE LEFT TO RUN.

BDEW!

BDEW!

ZZT!

TELL ME WHO HIRED YOU.

I MAY BE LOW-LIFE SCUM TO YOU. BUT AT LEAST I *KNOW* WHEN I'VE LOST.

YOU JEDI ARE *SO* SELF-RIGHTEOUS. IT MAKES YOU *SO* BLIND...

...YOU HAVE NO IDEA THAT YOU'VE *ALREADY* LOST. GOODBYE, QUINLAN VOS.

...

WHAT EVIL COULD COMMAND SUCH LOYALTY THAT AYO WOULD TAKE HER OWN LIFE TO PROTECT IT?

LOYALTY...? PERHAPS.

BUT *FEAR*...

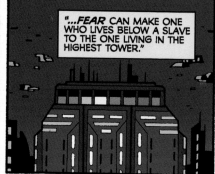

"*...FEAR* CAN MAKE ONE WHO LIVES BELOW A SLAVE TO THE ONE LIVING IN THE HIGHEST TOWER."

SIR, AYO MOROTA AND THE RED HAND HAVE BEEN WIPED OUT BY QUINLAN VOS.

GOOD. THEIR USEFULNESS HAD COME TO AN END. I KNEW QUINLAN WOULD SERVE A GOOD PURPOSE, HIS COVER BLOWN...

...VERY GOOD INDEED.

THE END

COME, JEDI... YOU HAVE BEEN EXPECTED.

EXPECTED? BY WHOM?

THE COUNTESS RAJINE, SIR.

OH, HOW I'VE WAITED FOR YOU, JEDI. HUNDREDS AND HUNDREDS OF YEARS TRAPPED HERE, WAITING FOR *ANOTHER* JEDI.

LET ME LOOSE AND I'LL BRING MY JEDI FRIENDS. WE CAN HAVE A PARTY.

*HA HA HA!* A POWERFUL JEDI WITH A SENSE OF HUMOR!

MA'AM, IF I AM NOT NEEDED I'LL GO AND POWER DOWN.

*WHIR-CLIK*

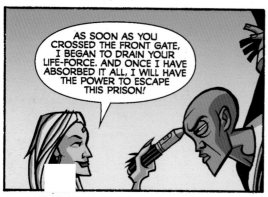

As soon as you crossed the front gate, I began to drain your life-force. And once I have absorbed it all, I will have the power to escape this prison!

You look tired. Don't fight it. Just give in...you can't win.

An energy vampire. I should have guessed.

Nothing more than a *parasite*.

Perhaps. But I'll live *far* longer than you.

Get out of my way, you junk pile! You're *always* in the way!

CLONK!

Yes, ma'am.

WHIR-CLIK
WHIR-CLIK

Come *now*, Z-18!

Yes, ma'am.

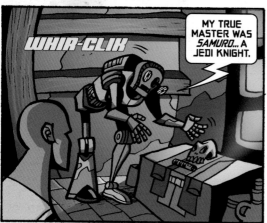

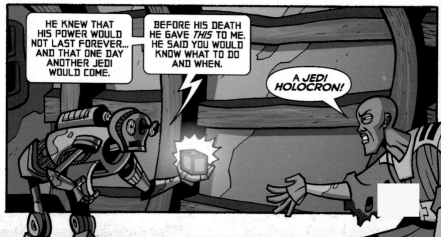

YOUR LIFE-
FORCES ARE
ALL FREE...

...EVEN *YOU*
ARE NOW FREE,
Z-18.

MACE WINDU,
REPORTING IN.
ALPHA-2 SQUAD
IS NO LONGER
LOST...

THE
END

# THE ADVENTURES BEGIN!

Star Wars © 2007 Lucasfilm Ltd. & ™. All rights reserved. Used under authorization.

## STAR WARS: CLONE WARS ADVENTURES VOLUMES 1+2

### FEATURING ANAKIN SKYWALKER, MACE WINDU & KIT FISTO!

# AVAILABLE NOW!

www.titanbooks.com

# EMBRACE THE DARK SIDE!

**STAR WARS: CLONE WARS ADVENTURES VOLUMES 7+8**

**FEATURING OBI-WAN KENOBI, AURRA SING & BATTLE DROIDS GALORE!**

# AVAILABLE NOW!

www.titanbooks.com